Only In Hawaii

Ann Kondo Corum

Bess Press, Inc.
Honolulu, Hawaii

Only In Hawaii

Any resemblance to persons living or dead is purely coincidental. "Hawaiians" refers to local people residing in Hawaii and not necessarily ethnic Hawaiians.

Library of Congress Catalog Card Number: 89-91801
Corum, Ann Kondo
ONLY IN HAWAII
Honolulu, Hawaii: Bess Press, Inc.

Published by:
Bess Press, Inc.
Box 22388
Honolulu, Hawaii 96822

Cover: Ann Kondo Corum
Design: Ann Kondo Corum and Steve Shiraki
Typesetting: Lines of Type
Cover Photo: Brenda Yonamine

ISBN: 0-935848-76-2

Preface

"Only in Hawaii!" How many times have you said that? Hawaii is like no other state. As the only island state, we are isolated and insulated in many ways. And because this is a place of diverse ethnic groups and cultures, we have a quality of "all-mix-up" charm. We hold on to traditions, but mix it up with the traditions of various cultures.

Certain things are very dear to islanders. Food, parties, and hospitality are among the most important. Much of what we do is tied to the "Aloha Spirit," a genuine expression of love, sharing, and generosity, given freely and graciously.

Hawaiians know how to laugh at themselves. As you read this book, you will see yourself and people you know in it. Why do we do some of the things that seem so silly to outsiders? I guess its because Hawaiians are what they are: sometimes silly, mostly unpretentious, often times innovative and creative, gracious, and fun loving. We have adapted to island living, put up with the perils of paradise, and do things that happen only in Hawaii.

Only In Hawaii chronicles some of our ways and eccentricities. I hope local people will get a chuckle out of this book, and that newcomers to the islands will get some insight into the way we are.

Aloha,
Ann Kondo Corum

DEDICATION

To all Hawaiians and the Hawaiians at heart.

You know you're in Hawaii when you feel "heavy air" and smell the scent of flowers when you step off the plane.

The continental United States (the other states) is referred to as "The Mainland."

When locals go on a trip, they take their supply of local food (SPAM®, saimin, Vienna sausage, corned beef) and a hot pot. Some people take rice and a small rice cooker, too. (No need if you go to Las Vegas.)

We travel with cardboard boxes (usually filled with goodies for the folks on the Mainland).

And when we return to Hawaii, we bring goodies home. (In boxes, of course!)

For inter-island travel, we use throw-away, carry-on bags (Portagee suitcase).

Hawaii is the only state where county lines are defined by the Pacific Ocean.

When traveling inter-island, locals always take delicacies from their island and bring back special treats from other islands.

Island Favorites

Oahu:	Roast pork, char siu, manapua, cakes from De Lite Bakery
Maui:	Potato chips, manju, cream puffs, azuki bean pie, protea
Kauai:	Cookies
Molokai:	Bread
Hawaii:	Taro chips, stone cookies, fishcake, chocolate-coconut sushi candy

We love Las Vegas!

Las Vegas is the favorite vacation spot on the Mainland for locals. Most Hawaii residents stay downtown rather than on the strip. These hotels not only offer the best travel packages, but here, locals can buy home-style food such as saimin, teri chicken, and Portuguese sausage and eggs. Also, they can buy "Hawaiian-style" beef jerky (made in California) to bring home to friends in Hawaii along with Ethel M chocolates.

Directions are always given in relation to landmarks.

Islands are basically round, hence, islanders have always given directions in relation to the ocean or mountains, and everything is relative to "town" (Honolulu). Basic landmarks on Oahu are Diamond Head, Ewa, Mauka (mountains) and Makai (ocean). What happens when you are beyond one of those landmarks? Name the next obvious landmark (Koko Head is past Diamond Head; Waianae is beyond Ewa). Also, use well-known commercial landmarks such as McDonald's, Zippy's, or Burger King.

Kona wind (a southerly wind from the direction of Kona) brings hot and humid weather.

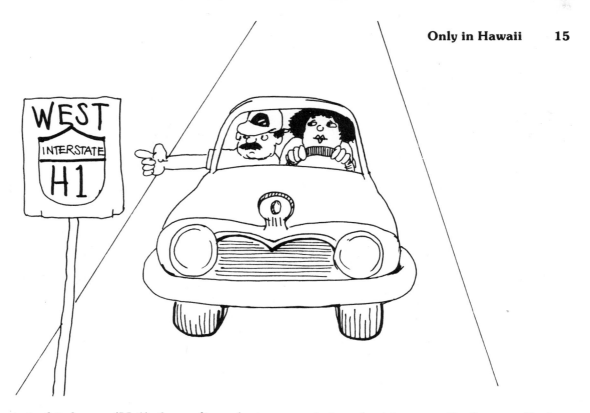

Our interstate highway (H-1) doesn't go between states, but is nonetheless called interstate.

So many drivers drive slow in the "fast" lane!

And many drivers stop completely on freeway on - ramps rather than merging with the oncoming traffic.

We love Hawaiian convertibles!

Pupus (local hors d'oeuvres) make a real meal in Hawaii. They are on the menu of any local party. Favorite pupus are: sushi, kal-bi, chicken wings, poke, crab legs, sashimi, won ton, macaroni salad, lumpia, and namasu.

Pupus don't mean carrot sticks and crackers in Hawaii. HEAVY PUPUS means no need eat dinner.

Opening day at the Hawaii State Legislature . . . the ultimate pupu party!

Official beverage of Hawaii.

We love SPAM®! Hawaii residents consume 4 million cans per year...3½ times more SPAM® than any other state.

And we love mayonnaise on everything!

So many kinds of chips.

Rice is the major staple of the islands.

Pork and beans and rice

SPAM® and eggs and rice

Bagoong (Filipino fish sauce) and rice

Macaroni salad and rice

Chicken noodle soup and rice

Tuna and rice

Kim chee and rice

Shave ice . . . everybody's favorite. (Ice shave to Big Islanders and sno-cone to haoles.)

Manapua is the local name for char siu bao (bun with pork inside).

Saloon Pilot

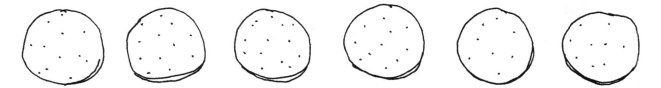

A "saloon pilot" is not a pilot who hangs out in bars. Known only in Hawaii as saloon pilot, this hard, dry, faintly sweet cracker has been known elsewhere as "hardtack," "ship's biscuit," or "calaboose cracker." Nobody knows for sure how the cracker came to be known as saloon pilot. Possibly it comes from the ship's cabin (salon) and the helmsman or pilot of the ship. Regardless of its origin, islanders love saloon pilot crackers. Try them with butter and guava jelly!

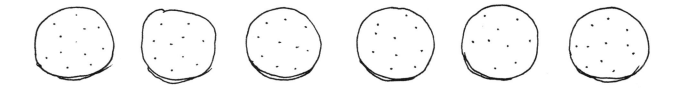

Chili pepper water (Hawaiian hot sauce). Mix together Hawaiian chili peppers, water, salt, garlic, vinegar and keep it in an empty ketchup bottle. Adds zip to everything from fried eggs to stew!

Lunchwagons are rolling local restaurants. They park near the beach, schools, construction sites, and industrial areas.

Our favorite lunch.

RAINBOW'S

HR'S

CHUNKY'S

Plate lunches are unique to Hawaii. There are infinite varieties: chicken katsu, teri beef, curry stew, beef stew, roast pork, pork cutlet, swiss steak, Hawaiian plate, spaghetti, chili, mixed plate, and much more. Note: plate lunches are always served on paper plates with rice and/or macaroni salad (fat macaroni with plenty mayo), and sometimes with chow fun. You can request gravy on the rice and macaroni salad.

KENNY'S

GRACE'S

MASU'S

ZIPPY'S

Loco Moco . . . hamburger, fried egg, rice, and gravy . . . a truly local plate lunch.

YUM!

Nobody knows where the Loco Moco originated. Credit is most often given to K's Drive-In or Cafe 100, both in Hilo. To make Loco Mocos at home, you will need hot rice, hamburger patties, eggs, and brown gravy mix. Place rice in a mound on a large plate. Fry hamburgers; place fried hamburger patty and fried egg on the plate with the hot rice. Top all with brown gravy. Offer seasonings such as ketchup, shoyu, chili pepper water, etc.

Hawaiian style care package.

Benefit food sales . . . an on-going local tradition.

TYPICAL HOLIDAY MENU
  TURKEY
  RICE
  SUSHI
  MASHED POTATOES
  KAL BI
  POKE
  FRIED NOODLES
  CHIPS & SALSA
  HAUPIA
  JELLO MOLD
  PUMPKIN PIE
  CRANBERRY SAUCE
  MACARONI SALAD
  NAMASU
  SOMEN SALAD
  HAM
  KIM CHEE
      SERVED
        ON
      PAPER PLATES

  BEVERAGES: BEER
           SODA
           LUAU PUNCH

Party time. All-mix-up food!

When we leave a party, we always go home with leftovers. When you are host, be sure you make enough food for leftovers!

Saimin . . . SLURP!

Saimin is unique to Hawaii. Nobody is quite sure of its origin. The Japanese think it is Chinese and the Chinese think it is Japanese. Whatever its origin, it is Hawaii's favorite noodle soup. Only in Hawaii will you find so many different kinds of saimin such as grilled liver saimin and Haole saimin (hot dog saimin). The best saimin has plenty "stuff" in it. You can put any or all of the following in your saimin: won ton, SPAM®, barbecue meat, chicken, shrimp, kamaboko, mustard cabbage, broccoli, carrots, bean sprouts, green onion, and egg.

Never visit a friend without taking a gift such as a pie, cake, cookies, fruit, etc.

We keep coolers in the trunk of the car to transport groceries . . . No need to rush home!

Haoles go to parties to socialize . . . locals go to EAT.

Sashimi is a necessity at New Year's regardless of cost.

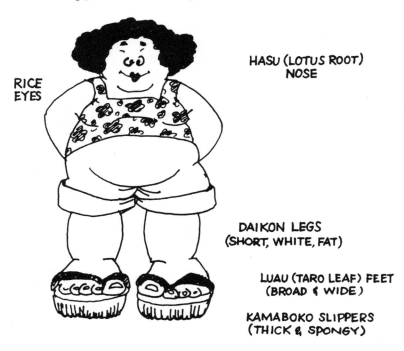

BOBORA (PUMPKIN) HEAD

HASU (LOTUS ROOT) NOSE

RICE EYES

DAIKON LEGS (SHORT, WHITE, FAT)

LUAU (TARO LEAF) FEET (BROAD & WIDE)

KAMABOKO SLIPPERS (THICK & SPONGY)

We describe people in terms of food.

And we describe food in terms of people.

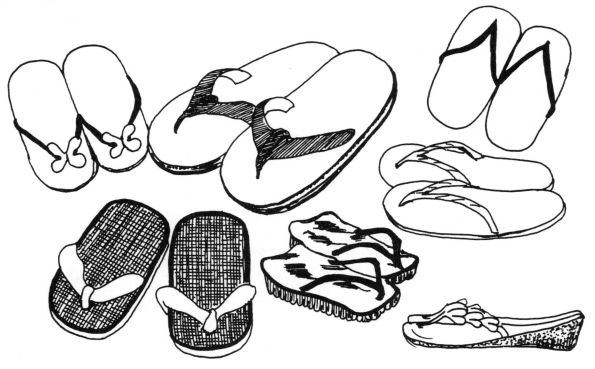

Official footwear of Hawaii. Be sure to take them off before entering the house.

We can run in slippers.

Guys wear shorts under their jeans (never know when you might want to go to the beach).

Little girls wear shorts under their skirts. (Some big girls do, too!)

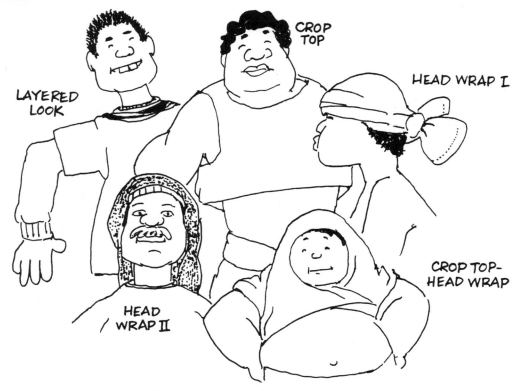

So many uses for the T-shirt.

When the temperature dips into the 60s, we drag out cold weather gear . . . socks with slippers, socks on hands, layers of T-shirts, hooded sweat shirts, and shoes and socks with muumuus.

LOCAL

SILKIE

POLYESTER POP

The aloha shirt is accepted attire almost anywhere, from funerals to weddings; from corporate meetings to cookouts.

TRADITIONAL

TOURIST

KID STUFF

The kind of aloha shirt you wear reflects your lifestyle and your personality.

MAMA-SAN

FULL FIGURE

SWEETIE

Muumuus, like aloha shirts, are the all-purpose garment of Hawaii.

TOURIST

NOUVEAU MISSIONARY

SEXY SISTAH

MUUMUU FACTORY

The beauty of the muumuu is that anybody can wear it regardless of her figure.

Because we are not a part of the continental United States, we often miss out on the best "deals."

We learn to be patient.

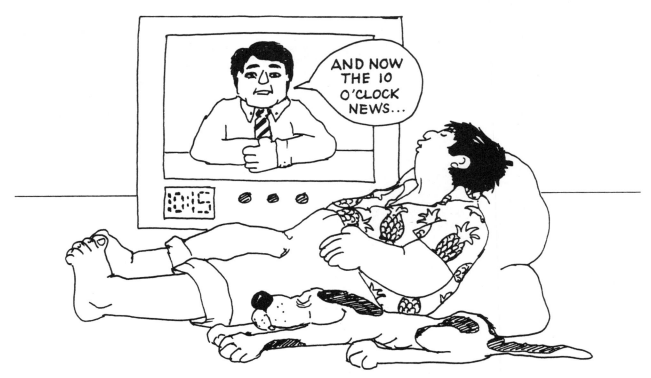

TV programs are on "Hawaiian time."

We see last week's national TV shows this week.

Our Christmas trees arrive just after Thanksgiving and are dead by Christmas.

Dogs and cats coming to Hawaii from elsewhere must remain in quarantine to make sure they don't have rabies.

The cockroach . . . Hawaii's state insect.

Cockroaches are one of the perils of living in paradise. There are 18 different kinds of cockroaches, some 1½ inches long. Some fly and all stink. Favorite landing pads of flying roaches . . . tops of heads and TV screens.

Cockroach trappings, a vital necessity.

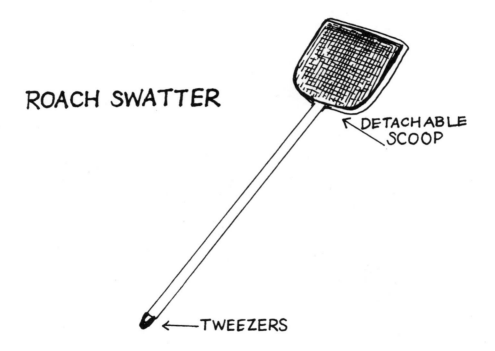

ROACH SWATTER

← DETACHABLE
   SCOOP

← TWEEZERS

For the squeamish who can't stomp roaches with their feet.

The *nene*, our state bird, is the only goose with clawed feet. Because it has lived on volcanic slopes for so long, its webbed feet have become claw-like so it can walk on lava.

The original "poi dog" was probably brought to Hawaii from Polynesia. This dog, called 'ilio, was fed fish, coconuts, and poi. Today, any dog of mixed breed is called poi dog.

Geckoes . . . a mixed blessing.

Geckoes are a part of every Hawaii home. They move easily over vertical surfaces and are known as the only lizard that can "talk" (chirp). Lizards were considered "aumakua" or ancestral guardians by ancient Hawaiians. They were friendly to the family that adopted them. Today, some owners of a new home wait for the first gecko to move in, believing that it will bring good luck. Geckoes help to control roaches, mosquitoes, and other bugs while making their own mess in your house.

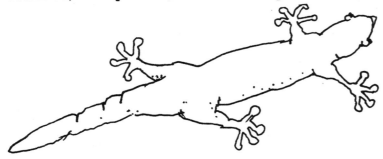

Hawaiians are great non-verbal communicators, and the shaka is a truly local sign of greeting.

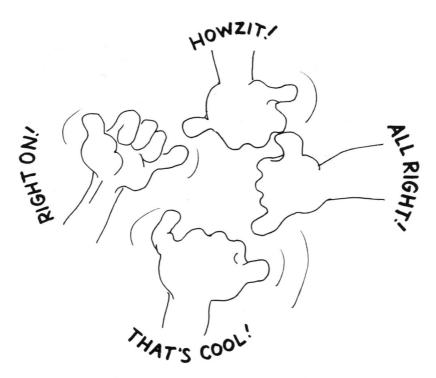

Greetings (howzit)...head bobs up, eyes meet, smile not necessary.

Stink eye (dirty look, drop dead).

Hawaiian-style political campaigning.

We campaign politically by waving signs and hands. It is not how well the candidate deals with the issues, but how well he waves.

There are three basic hand signals: shaka, wave, and thumbs up. When in doubt do all three.

The guy wearing the lei is the candidate. If you want him to lose, give him a hala lei.

Haole candidates: Be sure to use heavy sunscreen.

Beware of candidates with flashing lights on their sign.

Plantation squat . . . the best way to talk story, pull weeds, wait for TheBUS, or watch chicken fight. Note: only people with skinny thighs can do this.

Outdoor dustpans for sweeping up leaves and other garden delights.

We are the only state with a state song that is not in English.

A lei marks the memorable moments of life . . . it says hello, goodbye, thank you, congratulations, I love you . . . it says Aloha.

May Day is Lei Day.

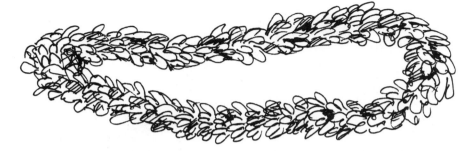

Lei Day is an island tradition. It is celebrated with parades, pageants, lei making contests, and the selection of a Lei Day queen and court. The first lei day, proposed by island poet/songwriter, Don Blanding, was celebrated on May 1, 1928.

We have so many aunties . . . (no need to be blood relative).

Our calabash cousins are not related by blood, but are very close friends who have grown up together.

Our rubbish men run.

Rubbish men (we never say trash men or sanitary engineers) work on the *ukupau* system. Under this system, workers are allowed to go home when their work is finished, regardless of the time it takes. The faster you work, the earlier you can go home.

We give beer to the rubbish men at Christmas.

We serve snacks to people who do work on our houses (roofers, carpet-layers, carpenters, etc.).

Locals always fight over who will pay for a meal (even though everyone knows whose turn it is to pay).

Liberty House sales are a major event awaited by shoppers.

Because we live on an island, people stock up on necessities (in case of dock strikes, hurricanes, and other disasters).

We have so many wonderful "mix-up" names!

We're proud of our heritage.

Baby luaus are a local tradition.

Baby luaus originated as a Hawaiian custom, celebrating baby's first healthy year. Now everybody has a baby luau . . . Chinese, Filipinos, Japanese, Samoans, and Haoles. Held in places ranging from garages to banquet halls, it is the highlight of baby's first year.

Hostess bars (a.k.a. Korean bars) are another tradition.

We never ask how old you are.

Priests are called to bless new houses, new property, new boats, and new endeavors. We also have priests bless a house which has had much misfortune or spooks.

We love to watch the world go by from a lounge chair in the front yard.

Garage party...

Hawaiian style.

We have the Aloha Spirit . . . friendliness, openness, consideration for others; sharing, caring, and mutual respect. It makes Hawaii what it is.

ORDER BLANK

Please send me _____ copies of ONLY IN HAWAII
@ $8.95 each*.

I am enclosing my check or money order for $ _____ ,
payable to BESS PRESS.

_____

Name (Please Print)

_____

Address

_____

City   State   Zip

*Price includes tax and handling charges. Allow 6-8 weeks for delivery.

BESS PRESS
P.O. BOX 22388
HONOLULU, HI 96822